Development: Journey through Childhood and Adolescence

CD-ROM for Windows® and Macintosh®

User's Guide

PEARSON

Boston   New York   San Francisco
Mexico City   Montreal   Toronto   London   Madrid   Munich   Paris
Hong Kong   Singapore   Tokyo   Cape Town   Sydney

Author: Dr. Kelly Welch
Developmental Editor: Mary Connell
Associate Editor: Erin Liedel
Marketing Manager: Carolyn O. Merrill
Production Editor: Michelle Limoges
Text Design and Composition: Denise Hoffman
Cover Administrator: Joel Gendron
Manufacturing Buyer: Andrew Turso
3-D Animation Designer, Video Producer: RocketBoy Studios
Voice Talent: Dr. Kelly Welch, Professor Dan Shea

For related titles and support materials, visit our online catalog at www.ablongman.com.

Printed in the United States of America

10 9 8 7 6 5 4 3 2   07 06 05 04 03

Contents

Development: Journey through Childhood and Adolescence

A Unique Learning Tool

Welcome to *Development: Journey through Childhood and Adolescence* CD-ROM by Dr. Kelly Welch! This multimedia experience will guide students through the fascinating process of human growth and development, where they will encounter videos, animations, audio clips, interactive pedagogy, and quizzes. The CD-ROM itself is a human growth experience—not only for the mind but also the soul.

Here we present Unit 4, "Beginnings."

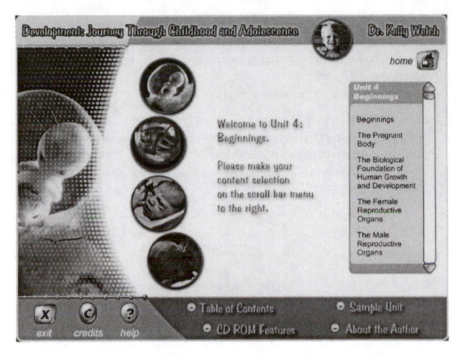

This CD-ROM is free with the purchase of a new textbook, or can be purchased separately.

Author

Dr. Kelly Welch is a professor in the School of Family Studies and Human Services at Kansas State University, where she teaches the large, introductory course, Human Growth and Development. Dr. Welch has received numerous university teaching awards, including the Presidential Award for Outstanding Undergraduate Teaching that recognize her enthusiastic, innovative classroom techniques and pedagogy.

"The videos are great. They provide students with a deeper understanding of children than they can simply garner from the text."
—Adrienne Sadovsky, Arizona State University

"The presentation of material is engaging and attractive. The video clips are excellent and exceptionally well done."
—Carla Goble, Tulsa Community College

"This is an impressive set of videos and animations—the pregnant body video was particularly helpful. A video is worth countless words!"
—Susan Nakayama Siaw, California State University, Pomona

How to Use This Program

When the CD is opened, you will be prompted to make a selection. All elements of this CD-ROM can be accessed from the main screen, or they can be navigated chronologically. Features include:

 Learning Launch Learning Launch is where students find the foundation of a topic discussion, such as psychosocial development in infancy and toddlerhood and cognitive development in adolescence. Points made in Learning Launch are often followed by illustrative videos or animations.

 Videos Each video on this CD-ROM is real-life footage filmed by Dr. Welch. It is life "unscripted." The videos allow students to see key course concepts brought to life and show how development affects children at different developmental stages. The videos also show how important education is when making life decisions.

 Animations 3-D and 2-D animations are used to illustrate many biological processes, functions, and changes. The 3-D animations in particular are an effective teaching tool because of their extraordinarily realistic appearance.

 Quizzes Each unit has multiple choice quizzes, consisting of an average of 10 questions each, or drag and drop quizzes, asking students to click and drag key terms into their respective "realms" of development (cognitive, biological, psychosocial).

 Mad Minutes This free writing exercise asks students to read a critical thinking question and on a two-minute time clock free write their responses without editing themselves. This assignment is helpful for capturing immediate reactions that can be interesting fodder for classroom discussion.

 Journal Students are provided with a topic or question to write about in a journal. They may write for as long as they wish, and they are encouraged to supply thoughtful and lengthy answers. Because the videos and discussions on this CD-ROM are designed to help students think about themselves and their own life, a journal will develop their thoughts and feelings and connect fact to emotion.

 Student Activities Student activities include drag and drop exercises, Web research assignments, and handwritten or drawn activities.

Glossary List and Flashcards Each contains a list of glossary terms and definitions that are mentioned in the unit discussion. Students may access the glossary list as a traditional text document, or they may use the **Flashcards** feature, which tests them on their knowledge of terms and definitions.

Table of Contents

System Requirements

Macintosh Installation Requires

Minimum Requirements

- 180 MHz 603e PowerPC
- OS 8.6
- 32 MB physical RAM free
- 800 x 600 screen resolution
- 256 colors (video quality will improve when monitors are set to thousands of colors)
- 56K or better internet connection
- 16X CD-ROM drive
- Browsers: Internet Explorer 5.0 or Netscape 4.7 (Netscape 6.0 or later: Users may experience some incompatibilities)
- Plug Ins: Shockwave 7.0.2 and Flash 5.0, QuickTime 4.0

Windows Installation Requires

Minimum Requirements

- 233 MHz Pentium II
- Windows-98/NT/2000/XP (Note: Win 95 OK, 98 and higher preferable)
- 32 MB physical RAM free
- 800 x 600 screen resolution
- 256 colors (video quality will improve when monitors are set to thousands of colors)
- 56K or better internet connection
- 16X CD-ROM drive
- Browsers: Internet Explorer 5.0 or Netscape 4.7
- Plug Ins: Shockwave 7.0.2 and Flash 5.0, QuickTime 4.0

Installation

On a Macintosh Computer

- Close any open applications or windows
- Turn off Virtual Memory in the Memory Control Panel for best video playback
- Set the Preferred Size of the application memory required for your web browser to at least 12 MB above its minimum
- Place the disc into your CD-ROM drive
- Open the icon for the Welch CD-ROM
- A window titled Welch demo will appear on the desktop
- Double-click on the "Start" file to launch Welch in Internet Explorer. If you would like to use a different web browser to run the CD, open the "Start" file from the "File" menu of any browser, or drag the "Start" file icon on top of any browser application icon
- Follow any onscreen instructions regarding your web browser's plugin configuration
- If you wish to install any required browser plugins without connecting to the web, quit the browser and run the appropriate plugin installer located in the Installers folder on the disc

On a Windows 95 Computer

- Close any open applications or windows
- Place the disc into your CD-ROM drive
- The Welch CD-ROM is set to autorun, so the program will start automatically after you insert the disc
- Follow any onscreen instructions regarding your web browser's plugin configuration
- If you wish to install any required browser plugins without connecting to the web, quit the browser and run the appropriate plugin installer located in the Installers folder on the disc

Notes

Notes

Notes

Notes